NOW, THEN AND AGAIN

ANANYA S. GUHA

Scarlet Leaf

2017

Copyright © 2017 Ananya S. Guha

All rights reserved.

ISBN: 978-1-988827-51-3

All rights reserved.

No part of this book can be used or reproduced in any manner whatsoever without written permission, except in the case of brief quotations embodied in critical articles and reviews.

For information address:

Scarlet Leaf Publishing House:

scarletleafpublishinghouse@gmail.com

Dedication: For my wife Punam and my daughter Anindita.

Acknowledgements: Some of these poems have first appeared in " Poetry Life And Times", " Dead Snakes", " Tuck Magazine", Vox Literary Magazine" etc.

A Poem

What is a poem, innuendo, dark spots in timelessness
what is a poem, rash, defiant, blood
what is a poem
colours, shades and those longings
of words to be fleshed
what is a poem
myopia, sentimental cravings of a world
to be eked out on blank paper
rattle of words
nonsensical syllables
utterances inchoate
the poem takes a stand
the poem is longitudinal curve
the poem a hiatus

Take out that word
in tightrope fashion
let it balance among vast seas
dead men and women, poets, writers, authors
rabble rousers, sentiment healers

What is a poem
you, me in black and white discourse
what is a poem
garbage boy, eating out of dust

The poem makes one last murderous assault
stains living, death
swirls in oceanic hope.

Blood

Rains prattle unceasingly
I speak, listen
to sounds, words, silences.
Spaces are infinite
so are wounds, these
rains are wounded
splendid drops
of blood...

City Of Cities

At a corner curled is a robust thief
in city of cities beside a mall
in city of cities.
Fictive city, city of imagination
city of cities.

In city of cities the walled fortresses
speak of new age, unbecoming light.
Guns rule roost, in city of cities.

Shaft of light
droning voices
dancing figures
apostates in city of cities

In waking night
troubadour of times
city of cities
you weave, a thin life
premeditated living
as arsonists and bombers
tear shreds of your life
in abject gluttony.

City of cities your riposte is
your will, silent answer to
marauders as you undergo face lift

breathing new life
into city of cities.
Rag pickers can only question.
Tormentor of times
city of cities!

Conversation

They told me don't
don't what I asked
don't shame (us)
don' what
don't what
I looked at don'ts
I didn't do anything
I only slept
I went to office
Don't My man woman alive
I didn't
sorry you didn't you did
I didn't
You did

write poetry

horse hooves
headless in Shillong.

I won't

Curfew

In the curfew
mist lifts
roads are besotted by stray dogs
policemen
and inside houses
the television waits
announcing finally of let up of hours

three more dead
situation is ' normal '
swirling around heads, in " sensitive " areas

normalcy has too many wounds and gashes
won't return so easily
needs to be hospitalized, along with the living

the dead need to be morgued
their memories to be written in graves
and they pointing accusing fingers at skies

the killers are guilty
of not killing more
the administration is happy
that things were " tight "

loosen, slowly from clutches of the dead
they need resurrection.

Distress Buying, Selling...

She sells fruits or is it vegetables
She sells on pavements, white washed houses
her coins ringing notes of sadness
She disposes of vegetables in evenings of skies
upturned
when volatile winter thunders.
She sells in a neighbouring village
her home, her point of no return
She sells in Shillong's bustling traffic
She sells she knows not what
her smile tells that she sells
and we buy, distress buying.
We eat. We haggle. We buy
and sing songs of praises.

She sells, distress selling.
We buy distress buying.
The notes emaciated, withered fingers
she continues to sell.
Pavements lined with vendors
lit lamps, when there is no light.
She sells whirling in scathing darkness

Dust

dust does not settle
it unsettles rovingly
it has movements
it wanders aimlessly
in houses, corners, books
and roads
the mind is dusty
when the rot sets in
the same questions, the same answers
the same love and hate, the same games
and the same killings.
here in India it is the gathering dust
over centuries, and history takes a new turn
hermetically sealed.

dust is soporific
dust is hermetic
dust gathers in oblivion
then strikes, impinges on ways of living, thinking
in this mad swirling we rotate with it till it sickens
with a thud around the corner.

dust is haughty religion
megalomania and a lassitude
kill them you morons in India
Syria, Iraq or Egypt.
dust has gathered over centuries in benighted
countries
so wipe it off your feet, give it a dash of blood.

bloody dust!

Editorial

You said: Poverty
there is no poverty
in this country
only slums and dilapidated children
snot nosed and education is a basic right
why it's even free like the
proverbial tree, kissed by the penurious wind
Impoverished are minds
minds that take off
minds that squirm with politico rage
minds unabashed who engage in paltry fights
do social work and then rove eyes
over glossy magazines.
No poverty, smart cities
will take over, ditties,
no poverty, only underdevelopment
makes, remakes everything here.

There is no poverty, only paucity
of rains, and farmers suffer
Learn a lesson from them.

Kill yourself, no brain drain.
Hit it, tear it, and sign petitions...

There would have been poverty
had there been no malls
and everything branded.

Yesterday there was a murder
No poverty.
Do you know the reason?
It was not poverty.

Event

The day passed off without event
events are happenings not on television
but events have suddenly dropped dead.
The day was unusually warm, sipping tea in a
restaurant
I summarized the day, the brutal killing in Uttar
Pradesh
is ghost lingering on day thoughts.
Events have manifesto.
They need to be signed, signed like law
they need sanction.
Is there any more?
What he asked?
Killing, killing, killing.
Not deaths. Deaths are natural. Killings are not.

Meditate on killings and events.
Who murdered whom?
Who though who was a pariah, an outcaste?
Who wants reservations in employment?

Events are a mortuary, when there are no (events).
They don't die so easily, but recur like the prophetic
ghost.
Their wraiths cling to bodies and souls
in a country delirious (with events).

The day passed off without event.
The day has not ended.

Evidence Has...

Evidence has that history scours past
but does not comment
history is archival
but does not comment
undoing it is reflection of bad moments
in nation's history, moments of regretful voices.

Evidence has that history unearths scalpels
and is conversation with present.

Evidence has history can become forgetful
if memoirs are in backwaters
and countries play with hammock and string.

Evidence has that history takes angular traffic to
berate
routes undefined to, admonish.

Evidence has that in corridors of history
there are wolves, but they have scripted meaning
to history.

Evidence has that monumental that it is
history is mummified when ghosts stare at it.

Evidence has that history rotates in time
taking long winded routes to oblivion.

Evidence has that history murmurs in winding
fashion.

Cerebral greats are part of it.
Songmakers.
Dreamers. Myth smashers. Idol breakers.

Divinations of quest.

Floods...

And then floods
catch us unaware
flash
enters rooms, houses
lightning strikes.
It happens to them
whose houses are rickety
life rickety
money, wealth rickety.
We wash our hands off- floods.
Don't be so cocky
Don't be so snooty
Don't you know it is natural disaster
especially in this nation, nay world
of flyover?

Wash your hands
Wash your feet
Pray so that you may understand.

Understand?
Relief material has been sent
the leader has taken a copter
a circuitous route
and saw
the floods.

Actually saw it through looking glasses
I will be damned if me obtuse as ever
could see through myopic lenses!

Flowers

Flowers withering
flowers deflowered, root out living
flowers come and go in changing seasons
flowers are reminder, a wish that this season
they will vanish like the spirit
flowers and the rain conspire to enliven things
and harp on many many things to come
such as events, love and blues.
Charismatic, flowers are colours,
marigold, hibiscus, jacaranda
their blooms give rest
swaying mildly at their best.

In wartime where are graves?
In death where are flowers?
Why do they dampen, then worsen?
O flowers you are a kind of doom
but in your colours we see, the prophetic;
wishes are flowers, handle them with care.

Look at vases, the metal
they shape the petal, and give flowers
their coloration. Hues. Flowers on roads
bristle with pebbles and stone.

Once flowers come and go
I am done.

Hands...

And hands which craft words
are responsible
for the blood which
rivets on streams
hands which hold each other
responsible for love a drudgery
and hands which dictate laws
responsible for death's shroud
all in one go
hands upraised
are venal, hands which pray
guilty of sins,
and hands are murderous
hands are sane
and hands which craft clever, witting words

are in a way hands
which are guilty of love.
Death blows hands move
in shadows, hallucinatory dreams
hands after all- in no man's land
heralding quiet platitudes.

History

They are baying for blood
blood the colour they have not seen
they have heard it is red
they want to foist religion
on the dead tree of a country
they are searching for blood
and catwalking with sentiment
upturning history, refashioning
it in glossy new text books.
Is history a mad man, runaway thief
to be quarantined?

They are now giving final touches
to history.
The history you never knew
never dreamt of
the history you never read
Now in dreams this will torment
till the ashes of a country weep.

I Am Writing A Poem...

I wind ways that lead to paths
I have traversed
I love it, walking I mean
talking of ways which are supple,
indeterminate.
We talk when mad, not sane.
Sanity does not control us
we are insane travellers
and when we write we are left
to mercies of insanity.

Calm down, this is not a debate
this is no psychological upturning
merely a poem discrediting the human mind
what else is poetry about?
Calm down I am in midst of writing
the somnambulist irks
the insomniac is a poet, within.

Outside mad dogs howl, moan, whine
it is their season of mating and dating.

Come down I am not lurid.
I am writing a poem-
To publish.

In Mornings

In mornings there is explosion
a certain humming, a certain resistance
to the sun or the thunder
cars frantic have rollicking fun
school kids think that morning is ceaseless
but, soon there will be shadows
and lingering dust
dogs' tail will wag
mornings are premeditated action
a little discernment
and mornings will take to paths
unscented.

In mornings
she takes her position near
the bus stand, vegetables that she sells
may or may not (sell)
but mornings are arcades of hope
and in this city mornings have the luminous
mornings have smell of flowers
mornings are creepy mirages of another day.

In Those Eyes...

In those eyes
a bird's nest
in those eyes shadows
in those eyes, incantation
song, in those eyes mellowed
tears,
in those eyes implosion, surreal
in those eyes we meet.

In those eyes the glow
aftermath of poetry.
In those eyes rains of yesterday.
In those eyes the mirror, shades
of a lamp. Infinite, in those eyes
your poem. Raven like
in those eyes your runaway hair
moist.

Inside The City

Inside the city
of hellish fire
a caged artist in fetters
scripts story
in silences bitten
by words

Outside the city
in hellish moorings
depraved people whip
mannequins.

Inside
Outside
the cat walks
the dog whines

All in hellish spouting fire.
Encircle, bring about rains.

Living

Did you know that in evening's storm
there is a puddle
and when you wade knee deep
torrents overwhelm
torrents undo do
till light emerges.

Do you know that alms of distress
are bittersweet
dreams.

Do you know, that in leprous hands
there is calamity
and in begging bowl for alms
storm is raised.

I go to do's and don'ts in weather beaten forgiveness
as cyclonic storm is only forecast.

Did you know, that in every praise there is
blandishment
and in every terror salutary hope.

All these I know in intuitive moments
some call it nonsense, I call it
ceaseless whirlpool of living.

Lord...

Lord I have read your word
when the storm calms I read
when daggers are drawn and blood is imminent I read
when the wind whispers in fortuitous truth telling
I read. When floods stalk houses, huts and tenements
villages and folks I read.
When friends snort, curse and pray
I read. Words.
I cup them in withered hands
and in midst of smoke and catcalls, brutal
bullying.
I read. Forget (to read).
I read your explicators
who swear by your word.
I read when the gnome dances
angels bless
fool derided
beggar humiliated.
I read.

Reading Lord is promise
I read in promiscuity
and money ridden torments
when a child whimpers with dog.
I read. Lord your prayers hurt, stalk
and reside in hidden torments
of time, myths and spoken word.

Man Dies

the chair angular look
the table plain but useful
the room ghost's prey
the hall, foreboding sullen
each is a man, animal
in midst of this there is refinement
table talk and coffee babble

till the chair falls
the table erodes
the hall crumbles
and
man dies

are they used for funerals?
no coffins are
are they used as man's memoirs, bibliography
yes
man dies
they are man's definitive symbols
man's wealth, and his tiny breathing space
the chair is comfortable
the table elegant
the hall silent, sad
man dies.

Mirages

Mirages are true
they are not mirages
we simply weave tales
we simply disconnect
mirages are everlastingly true
they tell a story
they are a fabulous world
mirages are punctuated with terror, horror
mirages are true, believe me

I saw one in ghostly fashion
and I saw one in dream
I saw one in my room
they are true, often they come
with dreams and somnambulistic
cat calls.
All blemished, all sullied
but they are true.

In childhood I saw this man
in apparent Buddha stance he sat
bald, grave, sitting in trance
it was I swear true. He vanished
out of my life

evaporating in Shillong's stillness
the bed on which he sat
was, is true.

Must I Not Write?

Marigolds in your hair
must I not write?

Tricks up your sleeve
must I not write?

Floods in your city
must I not write?

Your derelict homes
must I not write?

The breath of your living
must I not write?

Your waking dreams
must I not write?

Your dream hills
cherries blossoming
bite on your lips
must I not write?

Plum trees in your shades
must I not write?

Your breaking mornings
must I not write?

Circling in your water rush.
I must.

Obliterated Country...

In the dark street lights are nuisance
darkness is territory, don't you see?
a mad forlorn territory, it does not want
to be lit. It wants solitude of space
so that people explore its thin, masquerading
body.

In the dark, there is no wonder
no, what lives yonder, but only present
prescient. In the dark monkeys and maggots
play tricks with fire.

No upheaval, the dark is quiet, untenanted
it has no masks, it is dark, dark.

Walk streets of darkness
and in the dark there is penumbra
of old questions, terrifying answers
of a history and shores which are opal.

In the dark,
nights are turquoise
have pot holes, rat holes

a bomb explodes in the dark

exploring vast reaches
of an obliterated country.

On Reading Poetry

Turn those pages
turn them around
crisp, sounds words falter
turn them till words spring surprises
turn them till pages shrink into
yellow oblivion.
Turn these pages, turn around
will do the impossible.
Turn these pages, till smoke evaporates
and words are dream- reality.
Turn, turn oh dear, poems are frog- leaping
in every page
and the author rapid bystander

Is dead.

Prayer

They are killing people who are eating beef Lord
or supposedly
are they killing the animal or the man?
They are killing, not raping
which is worse?
In this countdown?
History must be sheepish, that its shores are tarnished
they are killing people Lord, who don't look like them
eat like them
don't wear the same clothes
they are killing people Lord
in this absolutism there is no crime
because they eat beef Lord
not vegetables or insects, in this killing
the butcher is cunning, the people are not weeping
simply protesting, killing people is not mayhem.
Everyday happening.
They are killing people.

So, they say ban this meat eating, worm eating, earth
eating.
Ban it, damn it.
They are killing people Lord.
My miniscule word, letter or poem
will not matter, what matters is slaughter.

They are killing people Lord in this territory
known for a long long past its history.
They are killing the past,
they are killing the present
they are killing the future
Dreams.

They are killing people.
Listen to this prayer
so that it bites you in your dreams.
Listen to this prayer so that kills you
in your sleep.
Listen to this prayer so that it may burn like
cataclysm
and stormy ghosts enter night dreams.

For, they are killing dreams O Lord.

Reading Banalata Sen

summer kisses brushed by the wind
you and I in love's embrace
outside the wind moans
and hiatus- of living.

three times he said
loving is not all about love
it is also how seasons and people change
react, talk, gossip and rains fall
on overcast skies. blues
it is also summer wine, winters blue moons
it is also rivers frothing, floods eating homes.
it is also humanity, tarred roads, infernal battle fields.

talking about love in a country that knows no history
is passionate quest, ancient, for timelessness.

reading Banalata Sen.

Refugees...

They come with the spring
They come with summer
They come infested with flies and pock marks.
They are despised
Their baggage is children, women
The men have no place.
They want new territories.
They are culpable
They could be anything, anyone.
But most important of all
they are refugees, seekers of change
as the wind billows
and storm screams
They are whip lashed by wind
and bathed with waters, roaring
yawning seas.
They are refugees.

Come me you let us go to relief camps
see their plight and write stories
media stories. Not fiction.

But fact scripted in graves.

Roof Tops

Roof tops are mad
rattling, whispering
groaning. They love noise
that is piquant.
They love silences of time.
Their lunacy is immeasurable
and then they chortle.
No, they are not humorous
their bland movements
are to be taken seriously.
And when rains pound heavily (on them)
they raise voices in chorus.
Sometimes birds, rabbits, dogs and monkeys climb
on to them in parasitical delight
when night's heaviness weighs on silences.

Roof tops then articulate movements
of steady sound. Rat- a- tat. Sounds
that impinge dreams, hallucinations.
Ghosts walk on them.

As a child roof tops hurtled into sleep.
Still harangue.

Seasons Change...

Seasons change
outside there is the odoriferous wind
outside me you are clamouring
calling past, rummaging dreams
outside you will be treading dreams
asking for benisons, from rain swept hills
punctuated by silence
and me you interlocutors
in the theatre of change.

People do or do not change.
They want respite in cataclysm of desire.
They want to love and then change
swirling in myths of a crashing world.
They are dilettantes. They know some love.
Some hate, streaming down rivers of bloodthirsty
change.

Selling Souls

Arraign darkness
those that speak
do not do
Arraign light, summon
somewhere, the gnome
sits immersed in philosophy,

And fools weep.
then laugh, murderous laughter.
They wait for final moments
on roof tops, and cataclysmic houses
as rot sets in. Their lives,
their philosophy.

Doing a catwalk
they sell souls.

Streets

Streets are lonely
as taking turn towards
eternity, they see lights
and stamp out nights.
Streets are war horses
and stones tattle on paths
streets gravel eyed, cemented
discern monsters one or two eyed.

Streets open out into unwavering folly
who knows
who are there?
24 hours in a day?
Streets host cats, dogs and men
as howling dogs watch ominously.
Go to streets when lonely depraved or mad
you will know how to feel sad,
in plaintive song
streets are inward telling
of calling, in midst of who we are
where.
Streets.

Streets...

I love to walk ways of serpentine streets
where people meet in dusk's ways
and where shops down shutters
because night arrives.
Still. Stillborn.
Lamps are lit and dogs
meet and then mourn.
Someone says bad omen. Death? Birth?
I love to see the moon in wonderment
and roads in grievous fault
whip gravels and stones.

Outside there is war, sniper and bullets
the big leaders talk of peace, rescue
how they have to save the race from bigotry.
Streets are silent, mesmeric in winds of change.
In the country, there are monoliths, grave yards
war. We love- our country.

Streets are in doubt. Questioningly they ask
which artefact are we destroying now?
which monolith?
where do we pray?
I love to saunter around a country
of history, passion, reason.
Dead will rise.
Graves will upturn dead voices.
Voices. My country.

In the streets silence is a way of life.
Babur came from Farghana. Made an alien country
his home.
My home.

Silence is outpour of past. In streets of Delhi. Dilli.

I love to walk in streets leading to hovels.

Summer In Fetters

The day was unusually warm
summer in fetters
September clad
the day betrayed illusions
of cold and the sun's glare
a bit too admonitory
the day shed off steam of summer
and embraced a nightly rendezvous
shops refused to close and traffic displayed
usual misdemeanour
By a lonely road walked a man
looked ghostly, waiting for a taxi
he reflected winter in perfect clothing
but the day did not understand that winter
presages warm clothes, with age it is a foregone maze
muffler, hat and woollens
and, swiping dust.

Tablet

Equipped with a tablet every day
I fight a rising blood pressure
the pharmacist asks for prescription
what prescription I say don't you see
blood pressure is common, look at the noise,
the ruckus on roads, the noise pollution
the bomb explosion, everyone has got it.
It is a common prescription for the common man
You and me, my wife yours...

When the tablet is missing, there is a void
like a loss, friend's death.
The tablet gets stuck in coat pockets, pant pockets,
shirts, trousers and blazers.
The tablet accompanies long travel, by foot, road,
air. When the wind blows fiercely the tablet fights
and hides in remote corners. What prescription?
It is a prescribed universal tablet with all this travel
running around, only to slink down the throat, like
painful death.

I rummage for it when clothes are washed
when lunch or breakfast is ready.
It is not a turncoat, turns up every time.
Any time.

The pharmacist, the doctor orchestrates a common
cause.
Fight for tablets. The armoury of both valid and the
invalid.

Ananya S Guha *Now, Then And Again*

The tablet fights a hundred deaths.
A hundred lives.
Stuck in coiled, tinsel, wrapped paper it breathes
perfection.

The kind, we need to live.

This Winter Time...

The wind is a holocaust
Memory seems mired
in spate of doubt
How many winters do we traverse
with the wind's reminder
and, darkness
Scalding nights will know
Dogs will know

This winter will it be different
as your eyes refuse recognition of the past
Is life light as you lie buried
in interiors of the self?
How I wish I were like you,
my friend, as this desire to search
is another moribund quest
Only poetry in this winter time
Can answer, stamped with
skeleton marks.

Time

against mad rush time is a safety button
you run against it, in strands
sands, clay feet
and then cutting across worlds of indifference
you see a new time, new way and paths to memory
is, what has not, what is
all will be taken into cognizance
where merger is fact
not tact or the fulsome moon
or the rotund goon
but time which is present
an ascent
against mad rush you create
delete, that hyphen- time
a rhyme.

against that mad rush
poetry may happen any time
rhyme, mad hatter
it is just a starter
measurability, mutability

in this mad rush.

Will Mists Lift?

Mist in eyes
you walk back thousand
times to memories
wrapped in dreams not coloured
but black, white
you walk back on streets that are lifetime
clouds of waste like rubbage.

Mist in eyes
you are passion of worlds
and murderous time.
Will mists lift?

You are waking dream
of an oblivion not far to see
and hyphen roads walk your dust
Will mists lift?

Spaces, time cannot answer
this history of life born;
several deaths will wrap around
fugitive time, moments
Will mists lift?

In winter, summer
paths are broken
songs of the city/ town
harbour a pilgrimage.

Will mists lift?

Send Me A Poem...

Send me a poem with calloused hands
or lines with Babylonian fire, Greek and
Roman myths. Archetypes of love lost
re born. Send a poem recounting man's
history of doubts, savaged battle grounded
fields, war cries and gnawing wounds.

Write that poem spouting lust
and stormy petrel. Write.
Send me a poem that speaks
of spouting hatred and love
awakened in marshy spots
promontories of time. History
ravaged, caste and birth marks
of Harijans, converts, dreaded minorities
neophytes. All in one go send me the poem
about a country's disillusionment and ravaged
beliefs.

Tear the umbilical cords, shred beliefs
you will know what time is and the written word
cocooned in hour glass. You may call it protestation.
I call it love of primordial time. Shards of time.

Wait...

Wait, there is death around all corners
even when the population is teeming
millions, then billions in a developing country
wait, the insane are sane, they want a rewriting
of everything. Caste, religion and colour.
Wait, the cities are going to be smart
towns will transform to burgeoning cities.
Wait.

Outside there is stillness, the pattering of rain
does nothing to arrest murderous claims, or doings.
In India there is no murder.
People simply die endlessly. Accidents, riots and mob
anger. It is collective herd mentality. Happens
everywhere.
Why blame a country and its people?
Wait.

The rain has abated now. Not the news, the news
pours in
like traffic histrionics. The news inundates our lives.
Cosmic force. Wait.

Yesterday I refused to read the news or watch the
television.
There is no use, the news will cackle out laughter, not
tears
on death of a person bludgeoned to death of course
because they say, his palate was of the wrong, wrong
choice.

Wait, in this serene afternoon hills refuse to be
bloodied.

We don't mourn. Only wait for the rains, the
whispering summer
wind.

My mind goes to poetry, fiction and protest.
I signed just now a campaign signature
while others put a stamp on death.

Autumn's Woes

Leaves, and autumn is picture post- card
crumbling, leaves will bite winter's acrid dust
he went to school wading through autumn leaves
crackling like fire flies, golden hued with smatter
of mellowed sunshine. He knew winter was to arrive
to penitential eyes. Unrepentant, he knew that light winged
autumn would colour days for brief respite. Summer winged
autumn to be wiped out as summer fruits would take
a toll.

Whispering truths, school would end and grey uniforms
languish in skeletal cupboards. Rattle unceasingly
the concert would end in brooding halls, with boys in grey green
doing somersaults to prepare for examinations.
The fire-place would make a beginning soon.
Autumn and its diurnal secrets, and the clock explosive
ticking away ruthlessly to stampede winter's storm.

Looking at these rains in autumn, I don't sight the leaves any more
they are downcast, in torrents, only past is what it is, searing, searching
dark ominous clouds are a leftover of floods, where numbers of people dead

are rituals in newspaper reports, many dead, houses
vanish with seasons.

Autumn is only one of them.
Let the past re-open in windows of childhood.

Poets

They are born out of a poem
they talk and weep
with words which stalk them
they are born out of ruminations
in isolated fragments of living
they think, then write with words
spilling over in light and darkness
poets, where does their starkness lie?
in prayers unmitigated truth?
in calls of the crow?
in ravenous forebodings?
I go to the poet when racked with pain
they have love, and desire for the up beat
they wallow in sorrow and imperfect understanding
their what is the where, the how and the beautiful
poets they come to us in unfettered understanding
of myriad images of the possible, impossible
poets
their hands and body are tired
tiredness and the self-wound bodies and soul
poets, go to them when dilapidated by life's
uneventfulness.

They will know what you mean
you will know what they mean.

You will be wounded by their craft.
Not hurt.

Never have I...

Never have I seen these rains
in mirrors of desire
or on the waylaid streets
or in the visage of a beggar boy
I have seen these rains plummet
down on rain washed hills
I have seen the rains whisked
away by runaway, embattled streets
and the pines look askance.

Never have I seen these rains
tepid, pale and wan
coming in torrents these rains
take away time and stupor
my languorous ways.

Never have I seen these rains
awakening anger
and a fetish lust.

Roads

I go to these roads
when legs are weak
walking is way of talking
silently in mesmeric
words. The roads unwind
past. no, don't call them memories.
They are wishful thinking.
Roads and walking co- exist
in myths and past. They tell stories
sing songs of blood and war.
Roads and walking are a tireless never
ceaseless endeavour
of stepping
of clapping
amidst waterfalls
and, whispering pines say
Roads.

And Outside...

And outside is murmur
of rains, the cyclonic storm
is making a heavy presence.
The rain persists gnaws at
memories, when with mackintoshes
we stomped ways to school
the puddles on the way
provided games and light entertainment.
The murmur is incessant, past and present
in dialogue. The dialogue holds
the pen wavers, the rains talk
whisper how eternity climbs slopes
of these hills with rains slithering down
roof tops.

I go to these rains in silences
I go to these rains with book
in hand, poem riveting in the mind
I go to these rains wondering how
these hills are washed green by
sporadic showers and outside
she sells vegetables, with umbrella shade
unwavering that these rains will save her.

The Afternoon…

The afternoon weighs down heavily
breathing, the afternoon is like a giant
snorting, as rain drops prattle on window
panes, leavening thought, setting aside fears.
But the afternoon also brings this yearning
of past and rainbow coloured roads, hills
with blue green hues walk across dreams.

It may happen anytime now- the rains
or the earthquake. The afternoon falters
as thunder clouds rumble and sleep emerges in
defiance.
The afternoon is changing course, meandering river.
The rains refuse to appear, only the wind sheathes
a cusp.

The afternoon is now asleep
cloyed with fears.
Lest it rain, lest the earthquake come.

Mapping A World

And the wind will maraud these antediluvian hills
a shudder, stammer as hills reel under a change
call it summer, spring or winter
but these hills glassy eyed will not change.
Inscrutable, myopic, walking through rains
of destitute. These hills are not metamorphic.
They denude myths and the ogre of being.
They have myths shrouded around them and photos
taken are at best evanescent. The hills have been there
since time, of a time, measured by time.

Serpentine roads lead to them.
Sometimes lined hutments greet them.
Sometimes flowers grow bedraggled greeting
them in hues. When colours fade these hills, their crescents
lift into oblivion. And then man cuts, sings panegyrics
on these hills, lush green, grey blue.
Children then sleep don't go to school.
Adults admire, sketch, paint and draw these hills
curious mappings of a nebular, infantile world.

When Evening Lies Comatose...

When the evening lies comatose
there is a making
there is a breaking of laws
saturnine thoughts
there is wistfulness
in making, when will it be night
there is a breaking of bonds- creatures are supine
there is how, why when
implosion, faces become masked
peel the masks
there is a waking
breaking
making
evenings comatose is malfeasance
evenings know this is ominous
evenings sob, thunder and then break
the earth into puddles of water
don't walk over then
don't.
hushed anonymity of evenings is foreboding
houses clamp down under covers of doors and
curtains!

Untitled

The cold mingles with the sun
outside there is a pause
sensation that something is not happening
the rains last night only came to delude
that winter hovers, it is already warm
the hills surround this town, and winter
lingers like the ghost on the run.
The highway is noisy and the road takes
a straight path to other unknown roads.
It is dangerous this highway someone said.
Accidents. Deaths.
And then those tea gardens- everlasting green.
Not a noise. Only speckle of doubt. Who works
there? Silence is a beast walking across dreams.
When will be go to see animals in the sanctuary?
The deer with the eyes which speak of history and
sadness?
The birds which float on ether?
The elephants which stalk mightily?
In the mighty river there is serenity.
In the mighty river, turbulence.
When will be going to see the animals?
The forest rangers are calling us.
Come.
Tourists come and go.

Wither's sun settles uneasily
into mists.

Another Season

Swirling mist,
the sun seeks
does not hide.
Autumn.
The lake is blue green
and celebrations are on
in this river- pine retreat
with hills seeking the aroma
of lifetime.

People are as usual chatty
line pavements to get a glimpse
of the morning or afternoon sun.
Only when the sun wanes will
they sit in huddles to discuss
the latest- people love to babble,
under trees or the sun
or the rains,

with a whiff of another season...

Summer Rains

These summer rains
are a whisper, not rains
the wet earth looks upward
and the soil breaks loose
turtle like. The snake climbs
up the sodden earth to discover
friends. Children ask questions
and play time will be over.

The sun dials tick ruthlessly
even as the sun wanes
and summer rains devour the earth.

I measure time.
Others measure hours
but like all creatures
summer rains are intransigent
huge metaphor of a living myth.

Ananya S Guha
Shillong, Meghalaya

Poet's Note

These 52 poems were roughly written between September to November 2016. I had just come out of hospital critically ill. The country was passing through a dangerous phase. History was distorted and, secularists were feeling isolated and threatened. An aged man was killed in a village in Uttar Pradesh, on grounds of eating beef. Slowly the secularist vision which the country stands for was crumbling. There were protests against this in leading universities in the country. Many students were hounded out of the campus. One committed suicide, felt that he was targeted, as he belonged to a lower caste, and was wrongfully implicated in a case.

The poems tend to make direct, angry statements, in order to drive home a ' message ' which many think is not in consonance with the aesthetics of literature or art. But art draws or pulls you into emotions. Look at the poetry of Nicolas Guillen. He strikes with words. I was going through an angry, hurt phase. The poems do the speaking.

Ananya S Guha

Afterward By Robin Wyatt Dunn

Anaya Guha is a delicate writer, aiming to please, and then changing his mind, and taking out his guns instead.

But Ananya only fires into the air; is it a challenge? Perhaps only for the sound of the gunshot.

A race?

Ananya's English is the English of the British Empire, still alive, still polite, still concerned, still incapable of doing what it most wants to do, because English cannot do that, must not, have what it wants.

Instead, it circles around, cycles around, tearing out its hair.

The colonial English of the British Empire seems especially concerned with misdirection, obfuscation, wilful ignorance, and Ananya is obedient to some expect to this regimen, but is aware of his obedience and wants to show the reader the limits of the conversation he is allowed.

But in the best traditions of a language over several continents, Ananya Guha infuses his English with the lush life of his subcontinent. In "flowers," we can see both the rich fecundity of his native Shillong, and the dual nature of these blooms evanescence: is their leaving an Eastern koan, describing some mystery of the spirit, or is it a colonial doom, pressing in on the viceroys and their adjutants, overcoming their delicate blue blood sensibilities?

Ananya Guha is aware too of his own status as a kind of blue blood, shielded from the poverty and the death and destruction of so many of his countrymen. For Victoria, the poor were unfortunates, bad cousins of that medieval courtroom drama in heaven sung in carmina burana, O Fortuna, and then of course this morphed into what we still know as a neoliberal / neo conservative Social Darwinism come again, of the poor as personal failures, deserving their fate.

No, it is none of that in the north of India, rather a deliberate blindness, like the Thom Yorke song, "this isn't happening.

But Guha knows it is happening; so what is the poet to do?

In Flowers, he is 'done.'

What is a language? What is it capable of expressing?

In 'History,' Guha measures the limits of translating the cultural experience of centuries into his colonial language. "Foisting religion on the dead tree of a country" is like his English, or part of it, the not-quite-sterile not-quite-healthy miasma of the men of India, wondering what it is they are allowed to say, capable of saying, needing to say, worthy of saying, doomed to say.

> *"the history you never read*
> *Now in dreams this will torment*
> *till the ashes of a country weep."*

Wordsworth is alive in Guha's writing too, and he can write in his mode without irony, something I would never be able to do as an American. Like Wordsworth, Guha "winds ways," in his "I am Writing a Poem," confident that poetry will arrive to him on his travels on certain footpaths.

But then modernity interjects itself with a kind of Freudian paralysis: *"Calm down, this is not a debate / this is no psychological upturning."* *"I am not lurid"* he insists.

Biography

Ananya S Guha lives in Shillong and has been born and brought up there. He has been writing and publishing poetry for the last thirty years. His poems have been published in " The Telegraph", " The Statesman" " Amrita Bazar Patrika", " Femina", " Sunday Mail", " Indian Literature", " Poeisis", " Brown Critique", " Poetry Chronicle", " New Quest", " Journal Of Indian Writing In English", " Kavya Bharati", " Chandrabhaga", " Poetry Chain", " Muse India", " Other Voices", " The Common Line Journal", "Fox Chase Review", "1947 Journal"," Leaves And Ink", " Muse India"," Up The Staircase", " In Between Hangovers", "Praxis Magazine", "Scarlet Leaf Review", "Kritya", "Glasgow Review", "Osprey Journal", "Indiana Voice Journal", "Shot Glass Review"l and numerous online journals/litzines/ poetry blogs in India and abroad. He is anthologised in several anthologies including the " Harper Collins Book Of English Poetry". He works as a Senior Academic in the Indira Gandhi National Open University and holds a doctoral degree on the novels of William Golding.

Table of Contents

A Poem 7
Blood 9
City Of Cities 10
Conversation 11
Curfew 12
Distress Buying, Selling 13
Dust 14
Editorial 15
Event 16
Evidence Has... 17
Floods 19
Flowers 20
Hands 21
History 22
I Am Writing A Poem 23
In Mornings 24
In Those Eyes... 25
Inside The City 26
Living 27
Lord 28
Man Dies 29

Mirages	30
Must I Not Write?	31
Obliterated Country	32
On Reading Poetry	33
Prayer	34
Reading Banalata Sen	36
Refugees	37
Roof Tops	38
Seasons Change…	39
Selling Souls	40
Streets	41
Streets…	42
Summer In Fetters	44
Tablet	45
This Winter Time…	47
Time	48
Will Mists Lift?	49
Send Me A Poem…	50
Wait…	51
Autumn's Woes	53
Poets	55
Never have I…	56
Roads	57
And Outside…	58

The Afternoon...	59
Mapping A World	60
When Evening Lies Comatose	61
Untitled	62
Another Season	63
Summer Rains	64
Poet's Note	65
Afterward By Robin Wyatt Dunn	66
Biography	69

www.ingramcontent.com/pod-product-compliance
Lightning Source LLC
Chambersburg PA
CBHW052123070526
44586CB00016B/2065